50 Marriage Vows

Men's Edition

Marcus Green

All rights reserved. No part of this book may be reproduced in any form whether mechanical or in audio form without the written permission of the author.

© Marcus Green 2021

50 Marriage Vows (Men's Edition)

50 Marriage Vows

This is not just a book about love; it is about the celebration of love. Traditional wedding vows have not been updated in a long while- probably since the days of Moses.

50 Marriage Vows is a two-part series: 25 vows in the women's edition and 25 in the men's. It allows each party to read the vows alone first. After choosing one (or more) of the vows in each book, couples can come together and compare. Each vow corresponds with the same number in the opposite book. This communication between each party cultivates and reinforces teamwork, a valuable asset in any marriage.

The vow that each person chooses should serve as an expression of their feelings for their significant other. It can be challenging to find the words to capture how you feel towards another person, so this exercise works to find new words and ways to express your thoughts and feelings. The chart ensures that each vow is presented in the correct manner and order, as it was written.

- **To my grandparents, Johnny and Joseph Calhoun**

"I pray that these books work as a tool to help you express your deepest feelings toward one another and to realize the importance of communicating and working together with your lifelong partner until death do you part."

- **Marcus Green**

Contents

50 Marriage Vows I

Magnificent and Marvelous 1

Why I Love You 2

Regular 3

Agape – Meaning Spiritual Love 4

A Woman Scorned 5

Relative Equality 6

Breathless 7

King Meets Queen 8

Who Am I? 9

Fasting 10

True Love 11

We 12

The Love of My Life 13

Forever 14

Where I Want to Be 15

I am Someone 16

Stolen Angel 17

Maturity in Love 18

Rich or Poor 19

A Great Choice 20

I Notice You 21

Rejuvenating Love 22

Risky Love 23

Art of Love 24

Lady and Gentleman 25

Prologue 26

Magnificent and Marvelous

Man speaks first,

I never used the word magnificent until I found you. In my mind, I dream of a million roses all weaved into a mattress, only shaped and molded for you. Where you lie in my mind is precious to me.

Your presence in my imagination is fabulous. I now visualize a place in paradise only because you are there.

I am deep into thought, trying to customize my dreams for your likeness. This has to be an immaculate decision. I pay attention to every detail and thought because they define your magnificent beauty. You are the source of my dreams of paradise; you cause me to have a beautiful sleep.

If I could live forever, I would make my dreams become my reality, and I would dream of only you.

When I imagine your smile in my mind, my eyes shed tears of joy. How can just your image make me feel so happy? I am content living in this dream world.

When I awake from my dreams, I must continue to daydream. My joy is found only in visualizing you.

How do I face reality and actually see that my dreams have come true?

Why I Love You

Man speaks first,

I love you with all my heart, and I will tell you why! Your innocence to see everyone as trustworthy and your confidence in human nature make me love you. You value people and give hope to all who know you.

I love you because of your overwhelming love and concern for others. Your caring heart that wants to provide for the needs of the whole world is precious to me.

I love you for your honesty; you can teach the most untrustworthy heart to believe in you. I'll always think of your dreams of peace for the whole world that allow me to imagine a better life.

I always think of your smile that lights up the world with your joy. Your enjoyment and appreciation of even the smallest things give life a new meaning.

I always remember these beautiful things about you because this is why I fell in love with you.

Regular

Man speaks second,

Every time I see you, I lose all composure and confidence. I am afraid to speak, struggle to form thoughts into words, and stutter before your beauty.

You are a wonderful blessing from God; what words are worthy of you? Our hearts and minds have become one.

As a man, I am supposed to be powerful, but my love for you overpowers me, and I am helpless. I disappear when I am with you. How can a regular man walk beside an angel?

I am intimidated by my love for you, and it controls me! You are so much higher than me. I am only a weak man trying to be strong enough for you, but you must lift me.

I am overcome by you! This weakness I feel around you that steals my strength has given me such pleasure.

You have softened my demeanor, and I am a willing participant! Without you, I would be just a regular man.

Agape – Meaning Spiritual Love

Man speaks first,

I remember when I first gazed into your eyes, my soul and spirit fell in love with yours. Our first touch felt like God had allowed clouds to touch my skin. I remember because I actually felt it!

I remember the instant passion that embraced us and threatened to overwhelm us. I knew then that I wanted it to last forever, so I gave in.

I remember the scent of your breath; it was the smell of ecstasy, and our memories overcome me because they complete my broken history.

This love is more than a dream; it's a spiritual love of two matching souls. This passion, this completeness, is hard to find. We have transcended the regular love between a man and woman.

We have become as one, in spiritual love.

A Woman Scorned

Man speaks second,

The pain in your eyes warned me that I would have to be patient with you. Although I could see how hurt you were, I could also see the strength in your personality. You are a powerful queen of divine beauty.

How did I know you were worth more than your hurt and sadness? Because when I asked, you gave me your name! You still knew who you were, and you never gave up!

You were looking for a man strong enough to fight with you and for you, to help you reclaim your true qualities that had gotten hidden behind the pain. You are priceless, worth more than gold!

I didn't find you, you chose to find me, and like a foolish man, I didn't know how much I needed someone as special as you. Was it karma or fate? I'll never know, but from the beginning, I saw your worth. I will always see your worth.

Relative Equality

Man speaks first,

Walk with me throughout this journey of life, where we will face our worries together. Take my hand and let me lead you to a place where there is no more pain.

Follow my love down a road where there is joy and contentment of mind and body, free from anxieties and doubt.

We will release our loving energy through long bouts of passion, and when we reach our destiny, we will be breathless. We are going beyond our sights and walking hand in hand towards our future.

So walk in amazement, strut like you are confident and proud of our love. I will not ask you to follow me, only just to walk beside me.

Matching steps and equal feelings, we will be equals. Let us walk together into our future, where being in love is forever.

Breathless

Man speaks second,

I am not your breath of life, but your breath gave me life; it is my reason to live. You are so full of life; the everyday things don't matter to me anymore, only inhaling and exhaling your love.

You are so caught up in loving me that you have forgotten the world around you. Being selfish is not an option you choose; loving me is the only thing on your agenda.

Who can say that they have actually stopped living for themselves to live for someone else? Selfishness is the biggest downfall in a relationship, but you will not allow that to corrupt us. You are kind, generous, thoughtful, and compassionate.

Sharing the same energy of love that leaves us both breathless; life for life forever.

King Meets Queen

Man speaks second,

We are in the beginning stages of success. This marriage means that we are aspiring to accomplish royalty and greatness in our lives.

No one can ever take away our success. After years of being in-and-out of deceptive relationships trying to find you, with my whole world out of balance, feeling hopeless, I held onto a vision of a royal family built on love, honor, and respect. A king and queen that would create a line of kings and queens. This royal legacy, we'll continue for generations.

Through our qualities of love and honor, we will create a foundation of royalty. I have chosen a queen that demonstrates the royal characteristics of wisdom, tenderness, unconditional love, kindness, physical strength, justice, and respect for all people.

Together we will guarantee a royal family dynasty with our royal children. I have found my queen, and she has found her king; now my royal family can begin to grow.

Who Am I?

Man speaks first

Hello, my love!

I would love to introduce myself as the one who will protect you, cherish you, honor your strength, embrace your independence, rely on your wisdom, support your ideas and dreams.

I will make sure that you never lose your passion for life. I will appreciate all your efforts, thoughts, and opinions. I will cherish your understanding, and I will be committed to you.

I will genuinely desire to meet your every need and want. I will always be that man that you were looking for.

I am the one you fell in love with!

Fasting

Man speaks second,

It seems impossible for me to eat, drink, or sleep when you are not around! When you're away, I must fast!

I am incapable of trusting or understanding the world around me when you are not here. When you're away, I must fast!

I am overcome by life's challenges when you're not around. When you're away, I must fast!

I stagger around lost and confused when you're not around. When you're away, I am condemned to fast!

My life becomes stagnant, and I'm unable to feel. I have no confidence, and I am afraid when you're not around. When you're away, I must fast!

Because I seek much more than just momentary happiness, I seek true love. When you're not around, I must fast!

I feel unloved and uncared about when you're not around; I must fast!

Your presence makes me feel alive; your presence feeds me. I abstain from everything when you're away; my life consists of only you.

True Love

Man speaks second

I feel tenderness and compassion every day from my partner. Accepting these qualities from the one I truly love is simply heaven!

I am fully committed to trying to meet all that your heart desires, just as you do for me.

Quickly responding to one another's emotional needs makes this life complete, and we would have it no other way.

Believing in our relationship is our true purpose, and we will remain content. We are each other's reason to live, and we urgently long for each other's embrace of true love.

We

Man speaks first,

We believe that we fell in love because of the joy we brought into one another's lives.

But joy can only take us so far, so we ensured our love by bonding spiritually and nurturing a much closer connection through prayer, shared beliefs, shared values, and allowing communication to be the primary building blocks of our love.

We have sacrificed our selfish desires and committed fully to the goals of love and friendship that we share.

We will build a stronger relationship by focusing our attention and interest on something more than just joy for a time.

As long as we can commit to loving and caring for each other as a team, there will be no I. Only We!

The Love of My Life

Man speaks second,

Do unto others as you want to be done unto you - the oldest lesson on love, the foundation for love to exist.

Because in my life, I have received unconditional love. My aura is love; my personality is love. I bring a character that is loving. I was built for this love.

I have been mentally prepared for this love. My heart can handle this powerful love that exists between us.

I cleared my mind to make room for all of these lovely thoughts, and I purified my body from lust, imperfections, and undesirable needs to be ready for this love.

Now I bask in nothing other than pure love for you. I see love everywhere; I don't close my eyes or blink in fear of losing sight of love.

The love I receive from you every day has consumed my mind and body with the joy of love.

Your love gives my life meaning. This love between us is not just a love of the flesh. You are the love of my life!

Forever

Man speaks second,

This relationship has been an uplifting experience for me, successfully reaching a level of love and affection that I never knew existed.

After many failed past relationships, you guided my heart away from disappointing journeys. Now, I am safe in the arms of love.

This relationship has given me the opportunity to rejuvenate my sincere passion for love. I am committed to this relationship forever.

We will share a lifetime of intimacy. We will build more passionate memories for each other in every single moment we share.

We have strengthened our partnership through the power of love. I have looked for someone as beautiful and down-to-earth as you, but your compassion and spontaneous nature are more than I could ask for.

Now that I have found my partner, I will forever hold you close and dear to my heart.

Where I Want to Be

Man speaks second,

I want to wake up every morning to your beautiful face and morning breath. When you come home from a long day of work, I want to run your bath water and surround the bathtub with scented candles for you to relax.

I want to rub your feet every day because you walk through this life with me, and I know I can be a pain at times.

I want to share ice cream and pie with you as we share our thoughts about our day through long conversations. You feed me, and I'll feed you.

I want to worry with you and figure it out together. I want to see how cute you are when you are mad at me.

I want to hear our names mentioned in the same sentence and be together forever. I want to be where you are and be in love with you for the rest of my life.

I am Someone

Man speaks second,

You are the power behind my strength. You are my motivation! You make me someone superior.

I am an enhanced version of myself, and I feel powerful. Because of you, I am a secure man.

I can be relied on if you need me. I can be believed in. I am in love, this makes me content, and I feel important.

I am valued and rich with your love. I have first place in the things you love most.

With you, I have the potential to exceed the best version of myself without you. With you, I stand out, and you make me feel like someone special.

Stolen Angel

Man speaks first,

I have crept up to heaven and stolen one of God's most beautiful, perfect angels. For this, God is mad at me, but He made a deal with me; I will not be held accountable and punished for my actions as long as I treat my stolen angel right.

I will worship the ground you walk on, cherish your beautiful presence, protect you from worldly ways and submit to your every need. You are my first and greatest responsibility.

I must entertain your mind with compliments, attention, and passionate words of love.

I must be truly sincere in how I feel for you, never contradicting my love by my actions. We will bless every moment we share by allowing God to be our foundation. Happiness is the energy in our relationship.

I must marry this angel and turn this bad into a good. For every wrong deed, I will make it up with a good deed.

It is my duty as your husband to fulfill my agreement, and oh, I will! I promise to be the guardian of my angel.

Maturity in Love

Man speaks first,

Like Romeo and Juliet, we can imagine that we are in a fictional love story that sweeps the world off of its feet. I secretly expose her honor to be faithful, a true queen to her king. Our imaginations merge to blur reality with a fairy tale.

We shared our secret conversation of intense suffering from desperately seeking each other. I needed you, and you needed me.

We overcame what we as people shouldn't be capable of by tearing down the walls of pain that tried to separate us.

We are allowing our love to surpass our ability to put each other first. We are fulfilling the simple principles of mature love. We are taking our feelings out of the fictional world of our imaginations and building our relationship on the reality of a love built on honesty and trust.

Our love is not built on the power of our sensual feelings that were never based on reality. This love is greater than any imagined love or fairy tale. It is a mature love based on mutual respect and self-discipline.

Our love is a mixture of imagining the best we can be and creating that vision in reality.

Rich or Poor

Man speaks second,

Our relationship is not a business that money should be taken into consideration; our love makes us rich. Riches mean nothing to us.

I would love you in a box under a bridge. I would love you in "hand me down clothes," with or without makeup. You're always beautiful to me. Without "Victoria's Secret," you're still sexy to me.

Loving and cherishing you makes me a wealthy man. I have an infinite amount of love for you. You are worth my time and effort, and I will gladly spend it on us every day.

I value your needs and wants, so as your husband and provider, I will ensure we won't live in a box under a bridge or wear hand-me-down clothes. The only value money has to me is to meet your needs

It's my job to protect you from the poverty of this world. I want to shower you with gifts. They say that "diamonds are a girl's best friend" and "roses make a girl's heart smile," but I believe that it is a loving and faithful husband.

I want to lavish you with the finer things of life because you deserve them, not because you demand them. Your sweet and humble spirit seeks only love. So I will always spoil you.

A Great Choice

Man speaks first,

My life was dark and full of desperate drama; I was in and out of meaningless relationships. You brought me instant peace. I have found a keeper in you.

You have calmed me down; indeed, I am deeply touched and changed. My very heart melts from the fire of our love. I have found a cure for my pain, and my heart doesn't hurt anymore.

Like a bird with a broken wing, I have been mended. Free from my bad choices, my faults, and the defects that controlled my thoughts and actions.

You have improved my thinking; you are my first good choice. Because I went with my heart, bad choices are now absent from my life.

You are now number one in my life. This first right choice has reformed how I make decisions and strengthens our relationship. I believe in my abilities again to have and give love.

I have been corrected, and I stand here today, awaiting those most beautiful words, "you are now husband and wife," the confirmation of my greatest choice.

I Notice You

Man speaks second,

Nothing will diminish how much I love you. Not the bad hair days, the baggie sweatsuit days, or a few chipped fingernails. Our relationship is not built on hairstyles or sexy clothes; although a physical attraction may spice things up and satisfy our senses, they are not our foundation.

Although your beauty was what I first noticed when we were introduced to each other, that was just our beginning.

We will always have the memory of our youthful beauty to keep us together as we grow old.

I love that you never stop trying to look beautiful every day. I notice your efforts, and I am drawn to the power of my beautiful and sexy wife.

My desire for you only grows, and I admire your inner beauty. I adore your charm that captures me and pulls me in. I am helpless before your charms.

You are so beautiful and sexy. I can't help but notice you, and I can never take my eyes off of you.

Rejuvenating Love

Man speaks second,

I'll be the one they blame and the one they label as a "bad influence." Oh, if they only knew that I only break the rules for you! You are my "Wild Girl."

Even though we are adults now, no longer youths, oh, your body can still make a fool out of me. Gravity has not coursed you yet. You are still beautiful, soft, and sexy to me.

I'm attracted to your beautiful smile when you're trying to show me you're interested in me. I'm attracted to your lips when they shake from desperately needing to be kissed.

Your beauty is rejuvenated every moment. Once again, I become that popular schoolboy, impressive and cool; the bad boy who is still innocent himself is just trying to win you over.

You were the most beautiful girl in the school. You can't blame me for trying to succeed in my attempts to win you. Every weekend we would go to the same movie theater, but every moment with you felt brand new.

You were my first feeling of true love. Oh, you shot my heart and made me feel alive, but the feeling will grow into a life of ever rejuvenating love this time.

Risky Love

Man speaks first,

I would gladly take the challenge to reach you and try to win over your love even if you were on the highest peak of the highest mountain.

I would run through the hottest desert with no water, swim across the blackest sea with no sunlight, and climb the highest mountain with no ropes. I would!

When I reach you at the top of the mountain and prove my love worthy of you, I would then fall to one knee and propose to you. Embracing you, I would claim my prize.

Together we will make passionate love with the whole world under us, for our mountain is on top of the world.

In my eyes, the reward is greater than the challenge. Why would I risk sacrificing my life for you? Because my beautiful love, you are worth the risk!

Art of Love

Man speaks first,

Our love is a beautiful work of art formed by the skill acquired from time and experience. We are people who know how to love and how to learn from each other.

We have perfected the ideal love, shaped by each other's feelings and founded in reality.

Our imaginations are our canvas, and we can paint the perfect picture of passion with our love. Our relationship is a piece of fine art—a masterpiece for the world to study.

Picasso was a great artist, but his work could only reflect the beauty of our love. Our love is like the sunrise and sunset; we form a unique vision of beauty.

We will not turn from this masterpiece to be lured away by a cheap counterfeit, neither turning to the left or the right? No, we will press on towards the true art of love. We will share our artwork with the world so that they too may know our joy.

Lady and Gentleman

Man speaks first,

I will open doors for you, making sure my lady goes first. I will throw my coat over a puddle of water so your expensive high-heels will remain safe and your beautiful feet stay dry.

I will pull out chairs for you and offer the last bite of food and drink to you. My manly greed will wait until you are satisfied.

I will finance every date and treat you to a good time. I will proudly say I love you in front of our friends and families. I will always make you feel special, no matter the time or place.

I will listen when you talk and pay attention to what you are trying to tell me. I will do things that you like to do, and I will put you first.

I will not let anyone or anything harm you. I will always fight for you and shield you because you are precious to me.

I'll remain the same - the man you fell in love with. I'll respect your wishes. I will even show respect to your father and ask for your hand in marriage. I will be a noble, gentle, proud, and patient husband, and you will always be my lady and my wife.

For you, I will always be th perfect gentleman!

Prologue

I am no writer, and I'm not sure I'll ever put my pen to paper after this first attempt. This book is a tribute to love and lovers everywhere in the world. I first saw love with my grandparents, and it was not like anything I saw in movies. Love is more beautiful, and the products of love… If I had only one wish, it would be to make everyone experience true love at least once in their lifetime. The world would be a better place.

I pray that you also find love – the kind that you deserve. I pray that you are loved back as you deserve to be loved. And I pray that you never lose sight of it because without love, what do we have?

www.ingramcontent.com/pod-product-compliance
Lightning Source LLC
Chambersburg PA
CBHW041809040426
42449CB00001B/20